T
TH

APOSTOLIC LETTER OF HIS HOLINESS POPE FRANCIS

APERUIT ILLIS

INSTITUTING THE SUNDAY OF THE WORD OF GOD

*All documents are published
thanks to the generosity of the supporters
of the Catholic Truth Society*

Cover photograph: Pope Francis during Pentecost Sunday mass in St Peter's Basilica in the Vatican, 15th May 2016. © Stefano Spaziani

This edition first published 2019 by The Incorporated Catholic Truth Society, 42-46 Harleyford Road London SE11 5AY Tel: 020 7640 0042 Fax: 020 7640 0046. English translation of Commentary on Aperuit Illis © 2019 The Incorporated Catholic Truth Society.

Libreria Editrice Vaticana Omnia sibi vindicate iura. Sine eiusdem licentia scripto data nemini liceat hunch Aperuit Illis denuo imprimere aut in aliam linguam vertere. Copyright © 2019 – Libreria Editrice Vaticana, 00120 Città del Vaticano. Tel. 06.698.81032 – Fax 06.698.84716.

ISBN 978 1 78469 625 2

Contents

Instituting the Sunday of the Word of God 7

Rediscovering the Word of God. 8

The Word made flesh 10

United in one body. 12

Responsibility of pastors 13

Christ: the first exegete 14

Sacred Scriptures and the faith of believers. 15

Scripture and the sacraments 16

The inspiring Word of God 18

The Holy Spirit in Scripture. 20

The Incarnation of the eternal Word 21

The Sweetness of God's Word. 22

Merciful love of the Father 23

Transcending the Letter 24

Mary's yes 25

Commentary on *Aperuit Illis*
by Archbishop Rino Fisichella. 29

APOSTOLIC LETTER
ISSUED "MOTU PROPRIO"
BY THE SUPREME PONTIFF FRANCIS
"APERUIT ILLIS"

INSTITUTING THE SUNDAY OF
THE WORD OF GOD

1. "He opened their minds to understand the Scriptures" (*Lk* 24:45). This was one of the final acts of the risen Lord before his Ascension. Jesus appeared to the assembled disciples, broke bread with them and opened their minds to the understanding of the sacred Scriptures. To them, amid their fear and bewilderment, he unveiled the meaning of the paschal mystery: that in accordance with the Father's eternal plan he had to suffer and rise from the dead, in order to bring repentance and the forgiveness of sins (cf. *Lk* 24:26, 46-47). He then promised to send the Holy Spirit, who would give them strength to be witnesses of this saving mystery (cf. *Lk* 24:49).

The relationship between the Risen Lord, the community of believers and sacred Scripture is essential to our identity as Christians. Without the Lord who opens our minds to them, it is impossible to understand the Scriptures in depth. Yet the contrary is equally true: without the Scriptures, the events of the mission of Jesus and of his Church in this world would remain incomprehensible. Hence, Saint Jerome could rightly claim: "Ignorance of the Scriptures is ignorance of Christ" (*Commentary on the Book of Isaiah*, Prologue: PL 24,17B).

REDISCOVERING OF THE WORD OF GOD

2. At the conclusion of the Extraordinary Jubilee of Mercy, I proposed setting aside "a Sunday given over entirely to the Word of God, so as to appreciate the inexhaustible riches contained in that constant dialogue between the Lord and his people" (*Misericordia et Misera*, 7). Devoting a specific Sunday of the liturgical year to the Word of God can enable the Church to experience anew how the risen Lord opens up for us the treasury of his Word and enables us to proclaim its unfathomable riches before the world. Here, we are reminded of the teaching of Saint Ephrem: "Who is able to understand, Lord, all the richness of even one of your words? There is more that eludes us than what we can understand. We are like the thirsty drinking from a fountain. Your word has as many aspects as the perspectives of those who study it. The Lord has coloured his word with diverse beauties, so that those who study it can contemplate what stirs them. He has hidden in his word all treasures, so that each of us

may find a richness in what he or she contemplates" (*Commentary on the Diatessaron*, 1, 18).

With this Letter, I wish to respond to the many requests I have received from the people of God that the entire Church celebrate, in unity of purpose, a Sunday of the Word of God. It is now common for the Christian community to set aside moments to reflect on the great importance of the Word of God for everyday living. The various local Churches have undertaken a wealth of initiatives to make the sacred Scripture more accessible to believers, to increase their gratitude for so great a gift, and to help them to strive daily to embody and bear witness to its teachings.

The Second Vatican Council gave great impulse to the rediscovery of the Word of God, thanks to its Dogmatic Constitution *Dei Verbum*, a document that deserves to be read and appropriated ever anew. The Constitution clearly expounds the nature of sacred Scripture, its transmission from generation to generation (Chapter II), its divine inspiration (Chapter III) embracing the Old and New Testaments (Chapters IV and V), and the importance of Scripture for the life of the Church (Chapter VI). To advance this teaching, Pope Benedict XVI convoked an Assembly of the Synod of Bishops in 2008 on "The Word of God in the Life and Mission of the Church", and then issued the Apostolic Exhortation

Verbum Domini, whose teaching remains fundamental for our communities.[1] That document emphasises in particular the performative character of the Word of God, especially in the context of the liturgy, in which its distinctively sacramental character comes to the fore.[2]

It is fitting, then that the life of our people be constantly marked by this decisive relationship with the living Word that the Lord never tires of speaking to his Bride, that she may grow in love and faithful witness.

THE WORD MADE FLESH

3. Consequently, I hereby declare that the Third Sunday in Ordinary Time is to be devoted to the celebration, study and dissemination of the Word of God. This *Sunday of the Word of God* will thus be a fitting part of that time of the year when we are encouraged to strengthen our bonds with the Jewish people and to pray for Christian unity. This is more than a temporal coincidence: the celebration of the *Sunday of the Word*

---

[1] Cf. AAS 102 (2010), 692–787.

[2] "The sacramentality of the word can thus be understood by analogy with the real presence of Christ under the appearances of the consecrated bread and wine. By approaching the altar and partaking in the Eucharistic banquet we truly share in the body and blood of Christ. The proclamation of God's word at the celebration entails an acknowledgment that Christ himself is present, that he speaks to us, and that he wishes to be heard"(*Verbum Domini*, 56).

of God has ecumenical value, since the Scriptures point out, for those who listen, the path to authentic and firm unity.

The various communities will find their own ways to mark this *Sunday* with a certain solemnity. It is important, however, that in the Eucharistic celebration the sacred text be enthroned, in order to focus the attention of the assembly on the normative value of God's Word. On this Sunday, it would be particularly appropriate to highlight the proclamation of the Word of the Lord and to emphasise in the homily the honour that it is due. Bishops could celebrate the Rite of Installation of Lectors or a similar commissioning of readers, in order to bring out the importance of the proclamation of God's Word in the liturgy. In this regard, renewed efforts should be made to provide members of the faithful with the training needed to be genuine proclaimers of the Word, as is already the practice in the case of acolytes or extraordinary ministers of Holy Communion. Pastors can also find ways of giving a Bible, or one of its books, to the entire assembly as a way of showing the importance of learning how to read, appreciate and pray daily with sacred Scripture, especially through the practice of *lectio divina*.

UNITED IN ONE BODY

4. The return of the people of Israel to their homeland after the Babylonian exile was marked by the public reading of the book of the Law. In the book of Nehemiah, the Bible gives us a moving description of that moment. The people assembled in Jerusalem, in the square before the Water Gate, to listen to the Law. They had been scattered in exile, but now they found themselves gathered "as one" around the sacred Scripture (*Ne* 8:1). The people lent "attentive ears" (*Ne* 8:3) to the reading of the sacred book, realising that in its words they would discover the meaning of their lived experience. The reaction to the proclamation of was one of great emotion and tears: "[The Levites] read from the book, from the law of God, clearly; and they gave the sense, so that the people understood the reading. And Nehemiah, who was the governor, and Ezra the priest and scribe, and the Levites who taught the people said to all the people, 'This day is holy to the Lord your God; do not mourn or weep'. For all the people wept when they heard the words of the law. Then he said to them, 'Go your way, eat the fat and drink sweet wine and send portions to him for whom nothing is prepared; for this day is holy to our Lord; and do not be grieved, for the joy of the Lord is your strength'" (*Ne* 8:8-10).

These words contain a great teaching. The Bible cannot be just the heritage of some, much less a collection of books for the benefit of a privileged few. It belongs above all to those called to hear its message and to recognise themselves in its words. At times, there can be a tendency to monopolise the sacred text by restricting it to certain circles or to select groups. It cannot be that way. The Bible is the book of the Lord's people, who, in listening to it, move from dispersion and division towards unity. The Word of God unites believers and makes them one people.

RESPONSIBILITY OF PASTORS

5. In this unity born of listening, pastors are primarily responsible for explaining sacred Scripture and helping everyone to understand it. Since it is the people's book, those called to be ministers of the Word must feel an urgent need to make it accessible to their community.

The homily, in particular, has a distinctive function, for it possesses "a quasi-sacramental character" (*Evangelii Gaudium*, 142). Helping people to enter more deeply into the Word of God through simple and suitable language will allow priests themselves to discover the "beauty of the images used by the Lord to encourage the practice of the good" (ibid.). This is a pastoral opportunity that should not be wasted!

For many of our faithful, in fact, this is the only opportunity they have to grasp the beauty of God's Word and to see it applied to their daily lives. Consequently, sufficient time must be devoted to the preparation of the homily. A commentary on the sacred readings cannot be improvised. Those of us who are preachers should not give long, pedantic homilies or wander off into unrelated topics. When we take time to pray and meditate on the sacred text, we can speak from the heart and thus reach the hearts of those who hear us, conveying what is essential and capable of bearing fruit. May we never tire of devoting time and prayer to Scripture, so that it may be received "not as a human word but as what it really is, the word of God" (*1 Th* 2:13).

Catechists, too, in their ministry of helping people to grow in their faith, ought to feel an urgent need for personal renewal through familiarity with, and study of, the sacred Scriptures. This will help them foster in their hearers a true dialogue with the Word of God.

CHRIST: THE FIRST EXEGETE

6. Before encountering his disciples, gathered behind closed doors, and opening their minds to the understanding of the Scriptures (cf. *Lk* 24:44-45), the risen Lord appeared to two of them on the road

to Emmaus from Jerusalem (cf. *Lk* 24:13-35). Saint Luke's account notes that this happened on the very day of his resurrection, a Sunday. The two disciples were discussing the recent events concerning Jesus's passion and death. Their journey was marked by sorrow and disappointment at his tragic death. They had hoped that he would be the Messiah who would set them free, but they found themselves instead confronted with the scandal of the cross. The risen Lord himself gently draws near and walks with them, yet they do not recognise him (cf. v.16). Along the way, he questions them, and, seeing that they have not grasped the meaning of his passion and death, he exclaims: "O foolish men, and slow of heart" (v.25). Then, "beginning with Moses and all the prophets, he interpreted to them the things about himself in all the Scriptures" (v.27). Christ is the first exegete! Not only did the Old Testament foretell what he would accomplish, but he himself wished to be faithful to its words, in order to make manifest the one history of salvation whose fulfilment is found in Christ.

SACRED SCRIPTURES AND THE FAITH OF BELIEVERS

7. The Bible, as sacred Scripture, thus speaks of Christ and proclaims him as the one who had to endure suffering and then enter into his glory (cf. v.26). Not

simply a part, but the whole of Scripture speaks of Christ. Apart from the Scriptures, his death and resurrection cannot be rightly understood. That is why one of the most ancient confessions of faith stressed that "Christ died for our sins in accordance with the Scriptures, that he was buried, that he was raised on the third day in accordance with the Scriptures, and that he appeared to Cephas" (*1 Co* 15:3-5). Since the Scriptures everywhere speak of Christ, they enable us to believe that his death and resurrection are not myth but history, and are central to the faith of his disciples.

A profound bond links sacred Scripture and the faith of believers. Since faith comes from hearing, and what is heard is based on the word of Christ (cf. *Rm* 10:17), believers are bound to listen attentively to the Word of the Lord, both in the celebration of the liturgy and in their personal prayer and reflection.

SCRIPTURE AND THE SACRAMENTS

8. The journey that the Risen Lord makes with the disciples of Emmaus ended with a meal. The mysterious wayfarer accepts their insistent request: "Stay with us, for it is almost evening and the day is now far spent" (*Lk* 24:29). They sit down at table, and Jesus takes the bread, blesses it, breaks it and offers it to them. At that moment, their eyes are opened, and they recognise him (cf. v.31).

SCRIPTURE AND THE SACRAMENTS

This scene clearly demonstrates the unbreakable bond between sacred Scripture and the Eucharist. As the Second Vatican Council teaches, "the Church has always venerated the divine Scriptures as she has venerated the Lord's body, in that she never ceases, above all in the sacred liturgy, to partake of the bread of life and to offer it to the faithful from the one table of the word of God and the body of Christ" (*Dei Verbum*, 21).

Regular reading of sacred Scripture and the celebration of the Eucharist make it possible for us to see ourselves as part of one another. As Christians, we are a single people, making our pilgrim way through history, sustained by the Lord, present in our midst, who speaks to us and nourishes us. A day devoted to the Bible should not be seen as a yearly event but rather a year-long event, for we urgently need to grow in our knowledge and love of the Scriptures and of the risen Lord, who continues to speak his Word and to break bread in the community of believers. For this reason, we need to develop a closer relationship with sacred Scripture; otherwise, our hearts will remain cold and our eyes shut, struck as we are by so many forms of blindness.

Sacred Scripture and the sacraments are thus inseparable. When the sacraments are introduced and illumined by God's Word, they become ever more clearly the goal of a process whereby Christ opens our minds and hearts to acknowledge his saving work. We should always keep in mind the teaching found in the Book of Revelation: the Lord is standing at the door and knocking. If anyone should hear his voice and open for him, he will come in and eat with them (cf. 3:20). Christ Jesus is knocking at our door in the words of sacred Scripture. If we hear his voice and open the doors of our minds and hearts, then he will enter our lives and remain ever with us.

THE INSPIRING WORD OF GOD

9. In the Second Letter to Timothy, which is in some ways his spiritual testament, Saint Paul urges his faithful co-worker to have constant recourse to sacred Scripture. The Apostle is convinced that "all Scripture is inspired by God and profitable for teaching, for reproof, for correction, and for training in righteousness" (3:16). Paul's exhortation to Timothy is fundamental to the teaching of the conciliar Constitution *Dei Verbum* on the great theme of biblical inspiration, which emphasises the Scriptures' saving purpose, spiritual dimension and inherent incarnational principle.

First, recalling Paul's encouragement to Timothy, *Dei Verbum* stresses that "we must acknowledge that the books of Scripture firmly, faithfully and without error, teach that truth which God, for the sake of our salvation, wished to see confided to the sacred Scriptures" (No.11). Since the Scriptures teach with a view to salvation through faith in Christ (cf. *2 Tm* 3:15), the truths contained therein are profitable for our salvation. The Bible is not a collection of history books or a chronicle, but is aimed entirely at the integral salvation of the person. The evident historical setting of the books of the Bible should not make us overlook their primary goal, which is our salvation. Everything is directed to this purpose and essential to the very nature of the Bible, which takes shape as a history of salvation in which God speaks and acts in order to encounter all men and women and to save them from evil and death.

To achieve this saving purpose, sacred Scripture, by the working of the Holy Spirit, makes human words written in human fashion become the Word of God (cf. *Dei Verbum*, 12). The role of the Holy Spirit in the Scriptures is primordial. Without the work of the Spirit, there would always be a risk of remaining limited to the written text alone. This would open the way to a fundamentalist reading, which needs to be avoided, lest we betray the inspired, dynamic and spiritual character of the sacred text. As the Apostle reminds us: "The letter kills, but the Spirit gives life" (*2 Co* 3:6).

THE HOLY SPIRIT IN SCRIPTURE

10. The work of the Holy Spirit has to do not only with the formation of sacred Scripture; it is also operative in those who hear the Word of God. The words of the Council Fathers are instructive: sacred Scripture is to be "read and interpreted in the light of the same Spirit through whom it was written" (*Dei Verbum*, 12). God's revelation attains its completion and fulness in Jesus Christ; nonetheless, the Holy Spirit does not cease to act. It would be reductive indeed to restrict the working of the Spirit to the divine inspiration of sacred Scripture and its various human authors. We need to have confidence in the working of the Holy Spirit as he continues in his own way to provide "inspiration" whenever the Church teaches the sacred Scriptures, whenever the Magisterium authentically interprets them (cf. ibid, 10), and whenever each believer makes them the norm of his or her spiritual life. In this sense, we can understand the words spoken by Jesus to his disciples when they told him that they now understood the meaning of his parables: "Every scribe who has been trained for the kingdom of heaven is like

a householder who brings out of his treasure what is new and what is old" (*Mt* 13:52).

THE INCARNATION OF THE ETERNAL WORD

11. Finally, *Dei Verbum* makes clear that "the words of God, expressed in human language, are in every way like human speech, just as the Word of the eternal Father, in taking upon himself the weak flesh of human beings, also took on their likeness" (No. 13). We can say that the incarnation of the eternal Word gives shape and meaning to the relationship between God's Word and our human language, in all its historical and cultural contingency. This event gives rise to Tradition, which is also God's Word (cf. ibid, 9). We frequently risk separating sacred Scripture and sacred Tradition, without understanding that together they are the one source of Revelation. The written character of the former takes nothing away from its being fully a living Word; in the same way, the Church's living Tradition, which continually hands that Word down over the centuries from one generation to the next, possesses that sacred book as the "supreme rule of her faith" (ibid, 21). Moreover, before becoming a written text, the Word of God was handed down orally and kept alive by the faith of a people who, in the midst of many others, acknowledged it as their own history and the

source of their identity. Biblical faith, then, is based on the living Word, not on a book.

THE SWEETNESS OF GOD'S WORD

12. When sacred Scripture is read in the light of the same Spirit by whom it was written, it remains ever new. The Old Testament is never old once it is part of the New, since all has been transformed thanks to the one Spirit who inspired it. The sacred text as a whole serves a prophetic function regarding not the future but the present of whoever is nourished by this Word. Jesus himself clearly stated this at the beginning of his ministry: "Today this Scripture has been fulfilled in your hearing" (*Lk* 4:21). Those who draw daily nourishment from God's Word become, like Jesus, a contemporary of all those whom they encounter: they are not tempted to fall into sterile nostalgia for the past, or to dream of ethereal utopias yet to come.

Sacred Scripture accomplishes its prophetic work above all in those who listen to it. It proves both sweet and bitter. We are reminded of the words of the prophet Ezekiel when, commanded by the Lord to eat the scroll of the book, he tells us: "It was in my mouth as sweet as honey" (3:3). John the Evangelist too, on the island of Patmos, echoes Ezekiel's experience of eating the scroll, but goes on to add: "It was sweet as honey in my mouth, but when I had eaten it my stomach was made bitter" (*Rv* 10:10).

The sweetness of God's Word leads us to share it with all those whom we encounter in this life and to proclaim the sure hope that it contains (cf. *1 P* 3:15-16). Its bitterness, in turn, often comes from our realisation of how difficult it is to live that Word consistently, or our personal experience of seeing it rejected as meaningless for life. We should never take God's Word for granted, but instead let ourselves be nourished by it, in order to acknowledge and live fully our relationship with him and with our brothers and sisters.

MERCIFUL LOVE OF THE FATHER

13. Yet another challenge raised by sacred Scripture has to do with love. God's Word constantly reminds us of the merciful love of the Father who calls his children to live in love. The life of Jesus is the full and perfect expression of this divine love, which holds nothing back but offers itself to all without reserve. In the parable of Lazarus, we find a valuable teaching. When both Lazarus and the rich man die, the latter, seeing the poor man Lazarus in Abraham's bosom, asks that Lazarus be sent to his brothers to warn them to love their neighbour, lest they also experience his torment. Abraham's answer is biting: "They have Moses and the

prophets; let them hear them" (*Lk* 16:29). To listen to sacred Scripture and then to practise mercy: this is the great challenge before us in life. God's Word has the power to open our eyes and to enable us to renounce a stifling and barren individualism and instead to embark on a new path of sharing and solidarity.

TRANSCENDING THE LETTER

14. One of the most significant moments in Jesus's relationship with his disciples is found in the account of the Transfiguration. He goes up the mountain with Peter, James and John to pray. The evangelists tell us that as Jesus's face and clothing became dazzlingly white, two men conversed with him: Moses and Elijah, representing respectively the Law and the Prophets; in other words, sacred Scripture. Peter's reaction to this sight is one of amazement and joy: "Master, it is well that we are here; let us make three tents, one for you and one for Moses and one for Elijah" (*Lk* 9:33). At that moment a cloud overshadows them, and the disciples are struck with fear.

The Transfiguration reminds us of the Feast of Tabernacles, when Ezra and Nehemiah read the sacred text to the people after their return from exile. At the same time, it foreshadows Jesus's glory, as a way of preparing the disciples for the scandal of the Passion:

that divine glory is also evoked by the cloud enveloping the disciples as a symbol of God's presence. A similar transfiguration takes place with sacred Scripture, which transcends itself whenever it nourishes the lives of believers. As the Apostolic Exhortation *Verbum Domini* reminds us: "In rediscovering the interplay between the different senses of Scripture it becomes essential to grasp the passage from letter to spirit. This is not an automatic, spontaneous passage; rather, the letter needs to be transcended" (No. 38).

MARY'S YES

15. Along our path of welcoming God's Word into our hearts, the Mother of the Lord accompanies us. She is the one who was called blessed because she believed in the fulfilment of what the Lord had spoken to her (cf. *Lk* 1:45). Mary's own beatitude is prior to all the beatitudes proclaimed by Jesus about the poor and those who mourn, the meek, the peacemakers and those who are persecuted, for it is the necessary condition for every other kind of beatitude. The poor are not blessed because they are poor; they become blessed if, like Mary, they believe in the fulfilment of God's Word. A great disciple and master of sacred Scripture, Saint Augustine, once wrote: "Someone in the midst of the crowd, seized with enthusiasm, cried out: 'Blessed is

the womb that bore you' and Jesus replied, 'Rather, blessed are they who hear the word of God and keep it'. As if to say: My mother, whom you call blessed, is indeed blessed, because she keeps the word of God. Not because in her the Word became flesh and dwelt among us, but because she keeps that same word of God by which she was made and which, in her womb, became flesh" (*Tractates on the Gospel of John*, 10, 3).

May the Sunday of the Word of God help his people to grow in religious and intimate familiarity with the sacred Scriptures. For as the sacred author taught of old: "This word is very near to you: it is in your mouth and in your heart for your observance" (*Dt* 30:14).

Given in Rome, at the Basilica of Saint John Lateran, on 30 September 2019, the liturgical Memorial of Saint Jerome, on the inauguration of the 1600th anniversary of his death.

Franciscus

FRANCISCUS

Commentary on *Aperuit Illis*

The Sunday of the Word of God

Archbishop Rino Fisichella

Commentary on *Aperuit Illis*

"The Second Vatican Council gave great impetus to the rediscovery of the word of God" This point can help us better understand the value of this Apostolic Letter with which Pope Francis has instituted the *Sunday of the Word of God*. In the half century that now separates us from the Council, a truly transformative force in the history of the Church, a fruitful journey was begun, that remains as yet incomplete, to bring the Word of God back into the very heart of the life of the Church. The events that led, following the Council of Trent, to the progressive distancing of Sacred Scripture from the lives of the faithful thus leaving it in the hands of a small select group are well known. Perhaps if St Jerome's saying that "Ignorance of the Scriptures is ignorance of Christ" had been kept in view, history may have taken another course. History however, is not made by "ifs" or assumptions but via the correct interpretation of the hard facts of reality.

In this context, Pope Francis's initiative acquires a historic importance. The next few decades will show how effective it has been for the Church and the flourishing of the Christian people. Some parts of the Apostolic Letter allow us to see clearly the Pope's aim and consider its value. First of all, according to a thought dear to Francis, there is the emphasis that Holy Scripture belongs to the people of God. Reconsidering the important points of the dogmatic constitution *Dei Verbum* and the reflections of the synod on the "Word of God in the life and mission of the Church" that flowed into the Apostolic Exhortation *Verbum Domini,* Pope Francis concludes that: "It is fitting, then, that the life of our people be constantly marked by this decisive relationship with the living Word that the Lord never tires of speaking to his Bride, that she may grow in love and faithful witness" (n.2).

And that is not all. He also highlights, with no wish to be merely rhetorical, that "The Bible cannot be just the heritage of some, much less a collection of books for the benefit of a privileged few. It belongs above all to those called to hear its message and to recognise themselves in its words. At times, there can be a tendency to monopolise the sacred text by restricting it to certain circles or to select groups. It cannot be that way. The Bible is the book of the Lord's people, who, in listening to it, move from dispersion and division towards unity. The Word of God unites believers and makes them one people" (n.4) This consideration calls to mind a similar reflection which Pope Benedict XVI made when he took possession of the chair of the cathedral of St John Lateran, "In the Church, Sacred Scripture, the understanding of which increases under the inspiration of the Holy Spirit, and the ministry of its authentic interpretation that was conferred upon the Apostles, are indissolubly bound. Whenever Sacred Scripture is separated from the living voice of the Church, it falls prey to disputes among experts. Of course, all they have to tell us is important and invaluable; the work of scholars is a considerable help in understanding the living process in which the Scriptures developed, hence, also, in grasping their historical richness. Yet science alone cannot provide us with a definitive and binding interpretation; it is unable to offer us, in its interpretation, that certainty with which we can live and for which we can even die. A greater mandate is necessary for this, which cannot derive from human abilities alone. The voice of the living Church is essential for this, of the Church entrusted until the end of time to Peter and to the College of the Apostles."

It is clear that this relationship helps us understand the importance of the Word of God which, being acted upon ceaselessly by the Holy Spirit (cf n.10), and through the constant interpretation of priests remains a living Word transmitted from generation to generation offering to all an answer to the great question of meaning that surrounds personal existence. So the Bible returns evermore into the hands of believers to feed and nourish them. From this perspective, the connection Pope Francis makes between the Holy Scriptures and the Eucharist, echoing that of *Dei Verbum*, cannot go unnoticed: "Regular reading of sacred Scripture and the celebration of the Eucharist make it possible for us to see ourselves as part of one another. As Christians, we are a single people, making our pilgrim way through history, sustained by the Lord, present in our midst, who speaks to us and nourishes us. A day devoted to the Bible should not be seen as a yearly event but rather a year-long event, for we urgently need to grow in our knowledge and love of the Scriptures and of the risen Lord, who continues to speak his Word and to break bread in the community of believers." (n.8).

In light of these considerations it makes sense to link this *Sunday of the Word of God* with the feast of *Corpus Christi* in which the Body and Blood of Christ are solemnly celebrated. This feast arose in the West in some way to question the Real Presence of Christ in the consecrated host. In 1264 Pope Urban IV, following the miracle of Orvieto, extended the feast to the whole Church with his Bull *Transiturus*. Thomas Aquinas took up the ancient work of Venantius Fortunatus (530–607), and composed the *Pange lingua* that remains to this day the Eucharistic hymn par excellence. The *Sunday of the Word of God* could in time be seen as an occasion when the Church celebrates the mystery of God who reveals himself speaking to humanity inviting us to a life of communion with him.

Three images from Sacred Scripture allow Pope Francis to illustrate the meaning of this *Sunday*. First, the well-known scene from the end of Luke's gospel of the disciples travelling to Emmaus. The evangelist draws a vivid picture of the disappointment and sadness of the disciples in the immediate aftermath of the death of the Lord. The traveller who approaches them on the day of Sunday is not recognised as Christ, yet he sets their hearts aflame when "starting with Moses and going through all the prophets, he explained to them the passages throughout the scriptures that were about himself" (*Lk* 24: 27). The Risen Lord opens the minds of his disciples to understand the Scriptures. This allows the Pope to affirm that "The relationship between the Risen Lord, the community of believers and sacred Scripture is essential to our identity as Christians. Without the Lord who opens our minds to them, it is impossible to understand the Scriptures in depth. Yet the contrary is equally true: without the

Scriptures, the events of the mission of Jesus and of his Church in this world would remain incomprehensible" (n.1). Christian identity is not linked to a generic myth that is the result of human imagination but to a true and clear story whose protagonist is Jesus Christ and that engenders faith. This is why Pope Francis writes "A profound bond links sacred Scripture and the faith of believers. Since faith comes from hearing, and what is heard is based on the word of Christ (cf. *Rm* 10:17), believers are bound to listen attentively to the Word of the Lord, both in the celebration of the liturgy and in their personal prayer and reflection" (n.7).

A second image is taken from the story told by the book of Nehemiah of the return of the people from exile and the emotion felt as a result of the rediscovery and rereading of the sacred texts. From here we learn and discover anew that we can gather as a united and joyful people around the Word of the Lord, without being overwhelmed by the richness it contains but rather being pushed onward to make as yet unknown discoveries in it. Quoting from the beautiful text of the saint, poet and theologian Ephrem the Syrian (306–373) allows the Pope to present the Word of God as an eternal, deep and inexhaustible fountain. With the same words as the Syrian deacon, we can affirm "Rejoice for you have been filled, do not be sad on seeing that the richness of the word is far beyond you. If you are thirsty you are glad to drink and are not saddened that you are unable to drain the fountain. It is better that the fountain quenches your thirst than that your thirst exhausts the fountain. If your thirst is slaked without the fountain drying up, you can drink of it each time you have need. If instead, by drinking your fill you dried up the stream, your achievement would be your tragedy. Be thankful for what you have received and do not grumble about what remains unused. What you have taken or carried away with you is now yours but what remains is yet your future inheritance. What you have been unable to receive immediately because you are weak, you can receive at another time thanks to your perseverance" (*Commentary on the Diatessaron*). Following this teaching, Pope Francis is once again working to understand the needs of the people of God, so that priests may be good and faithful preachers in their homilies. This is a theme particularly dear to the Pope which he has many times wished to underscore and he does so again here "The homily, in particular, has a distinctive function… For many of our faithful, in fact, this is the only opportunity they have to grasp the beauty of God's Word and to see it applied to their daily lives…Those of us who are preachers should not give long, pedantic homilies or wander off into unrelated topics. When we take time to pray and meditate on the sacred text, we can speak from the heart and thus reach the hearts of those who hear us, conveying what is essential and capable of bearing fruit" (n.5).

The last image draws on two texts, from the prophet Ezekiel (cf. 3:3) and from Revelation (cf. 10:10) where the Word of God is shown in its sweetness and its bitterness. Pope Francis uses this teaching to affirm that Sacred Scripture carries out a truly "prophetic work" (n.12). Guided by the Holy Spirit in fact, we learn that not only did that same Spirit inspire the sacred authors but that he acts in all those "who hear the word of God." (n.10). The dynamic and living character of the Word of God cannot therefore be shut up in a book, but transcends it as a living announcement, making the Church a people with the responsibility of passing on, without pause and until the end of time, the Word which brought her forth and leads to her fulfilment; a Word moreover which is as sweet as honey when heard but sour when it reaches the stomach. Pope Francis's words deal specifically with this vision: "The sweetness of God's word leads us to share it with all those whom we encounter in this life and to proclaim the sure hope that it contains (cf. *1 P* 3:15-16). Its bitterness, in turn, often comes from our realisation of how difficult it is to live that Word consistently, or our personal experience of seeing it rejected as meaningless for life" (n.12).

The *Sunday of the Word of God* is a real opportunity offered to our communities to strengthen what is ongoing and tirelessly go further without ever getting too accustomed to the newness that it presents us with. Pope Francis recognises that many initiatives are already present in local churches and yet the coming together on one *Sunday*, as a sign of unity and ecumenical action, can favour a deeper understanding of the Bible and wider knowledge of it amongst believers (cf. n.3). It is a pastoral opportunity to strengthen the enthusiasm for the new evangelisation which is the work of the faithful in this historical moment full of challenges to which the Word of God is a meaningful solution.

✠ His Excellency Mgr Rino Fisichella
President of the Pontifical Council for the Promotion of the New Evangelisation